FANTASTICALLY FUNNY

500 SILLY JOKES!

PaRragon

Bath · New York · Cologne · Melbourne · Delhi
Hong Kong · Shenzhen · Singapore

This edition published by Parragon Books Ltd in 2018

Parragon Books Ltd
Chartist House
15–17 Trim Street
Bath BA1 1HA, UK
www.parragon.com

Designed by Lauren Tiley
Edited by Emma Horridge
Production by Jon Wakeham

ISBN 978-1-5270-0999-8

Printed in China

CONTENTS

ANIMALS

What's the difference between a teenager and a leopard?
One's covered in spots and sleeps all day, and the other is a leopard.

What's an elephant's favourite sport?
Squash.

What's green with red spots?
A frog with chicken pox.

What looks like half a cat?
The other half.

Where do monkeys hear rumours?
On the apevine.

Which eel invaded Britain?
William the Conger.

Why did the bees go on strike?
For more honey and shorter flowers.

Toby: How would you feel if you saw a dinosaur in your garden?
Tyler: Very old!

When do mice follow cats?
In a dictionary.

Which cat discovered America?
Christopher Colum-puss.

What do you call a dog with a cold?
A-choo-wawa.

When are most frogs born?
In a leap year.

What happens when a dog, a tap and a tomato enter a race?
Well, the dog is in the lead, the tap is running and the tomato is trying to ketchup.

How do you know if there is an elephant under your bed?
Your nose is touching the ceiling.

Why do cows wear bells?
Because their horns don't work.

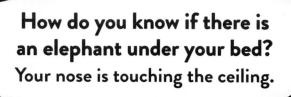

What happened to the frog that parked on double yellow lines?
He was toad away.

What do porcupines say when they hug?
Ouch!

What's a lion's favourite day of the week?
Chews-day.

What do you get if you cross an elephant with a whale?
A submarine with a built-in snorkel.

Who's the penguin's favourite aunt?
Aunt-arctica.

What do you get if you cross a snake with a digger?
A boa constructor.

10

What do you get if you cross a cat with a surgeon?
A doctor-puss.

What would happen if worms took over the planet?
Global worming.

What do you get if you cross a dog with a phone?
A golden receiver.

11

Why did the cat stop talking?
There was a paws in the conversation.

What do you get if you cross a duck with a box of matches?
A fire-quacker.

Which snakes are best at maths?
Adders.

How do you take a lion's temperature?
Very carefully!

What did dinosaurs have that no other animals ever had?
Baby dinosaurs.

What do you get if you cross a kangaroo with a triceratops?
A tricera-hops.

What's green and dangerous?
A frog with a gun.

Why did the cow cross the road?
To get to the udder side.

WRITE YOUR OWN QUACKY JOKE...

Charlie: I was arrested for stealing a pig.
Ben: How did they catch you?
Charlie: The pig squealed.

What do you call a dinosaur that never gives up?
A try, try, try-ceratops.

How do you stop a dog barking in the back seat of a car?
Put him in the front seat.

What says 'quick, quick'?
A duck with hiccups.

Why did the chewing gum cross the road?
Because it was stuck to the chicken's foot.

It's raining cats and dogs!
I know, I just stepped in a poodle.

Why doesn't Sweden export its cattle?
Because it wants to keep its Stockholm.

16

What do you do with a sick horse?
Take it to hors-pital.

What does a crab use to call its friends?
A shellphone.

Which pets make the most noise?
Trumpets.

Why don't penguins carry fish in their pockets?
Because they don't have pockets.

17

19

What do you get if you cross
a cow with a grass cutter?

A lawn mooer.

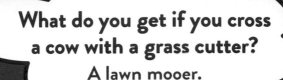

Why are penguins
good race car drivers?

Because they're always
in pole position.

What do you call a bee that
is always complaining?

A grumble bee.

What kind of key
can't open a lock?

A don-key.

WRITE A JOKE AND LAUGH LIKE A DONKEY...

Which cheese do mice love the most?
Mouse-erella.

What do dinosaurs use to cut down trees?
Dinosaws.

Why are penguins so popular on the internet?
Because they have web feet.

What do you get if you cross a polar bear with a flower?
I don't know, but I'm not going to smell it.

22

Why didn't the sea creatures
understand each other?
They were speaking at
cross porpoises.

Why was the baby
ant so confused?
Because all its
uncles were ants.

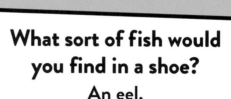

What sort of fish would
you find in a shoe?
An eel.

What do you call
a flock of chickens
crossing the road?
Poultry in motion.

What do you get when you cross a fish with an elephant? Swimming trunks.

What do you call a dinosaur with blisters? My-feet-are-sore-us.

What do whales chew? Blubber gum.

Why did the chick footballer get a yellow card? He committed a fowl.

25

Why didn't the
dinosaur cross the road?
There weren't any roads
in those days.

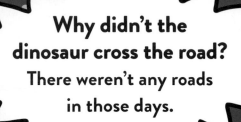

Which side of a cat
has the most fur?
The outside.

How do baby bees
get to school?
On a school buzz.

Why did the chicken
cross the web?
To get to the
other site.

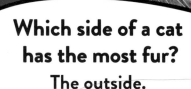

How do cats
end an argument?
They hiss and
make up.

What's the difference
between a piano
and a fish?
You can tune a piano,
but you can't tuna fish.

Which insect keeps
running away?
The flee!

What do you give a
pony with a cold?
Cough stirrup.

What do you call a
terrified dinosaur?
Nervous Rex.

Did you hear about
the cat that swallowed
a ball of wool?
She had mittens.

What do you get
when you cross a parrot
with a centipede?
A walkie-talkie.

What do you call a dinosaur
that complains all the time?
A whine-osaur.

What do you get if you
cross a duck with a rooster?
A bird that wakes you up
at the quack of dawn.

Where do fish wash?
In a river basin.

What is leafy, green and sings? Elvis Parsley.

What do elves make sandwiches with? Shortbread.

What is a pretzel's favourite dance? The twist.

What do you call a peanut in a spacesuit? An astro-nut.

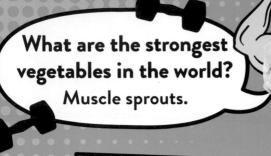

What are the strongest vegetables in the world?
Muscle sprouts.

What's the best way to see flying saucers?
Trip up the waiter.

Waiter, will my pizza be long?
No, it'll be round, the same as everyone else's!

How did the farmer repair his jeans?
With a vegetable patch.

Why did the strawberry cry?
Because his friends were in a jam.

How do you make fairy cakes?
With elf-raising flour.

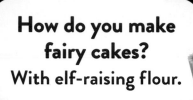

What's white and swings through the jungle?
A meringue-utan.

Did you hear the terrible egg joke?
It wasn't all it was cracked up to be.

What's the most popular pudding in France?
The trifle tower.

Why did the lettuce blush?
He saw the salad dressing.

What sits in the corner of the room and wobbles?
A jelly-vision.

How does a penguin make pancakes?
With its flippers.

What happened to the man who stole an apple pie?
He was taken into custard-y.

Mum: Eat your spinach, it'll put colour in your cheeks.

Max: But I don't want green cheeks!

What did the tomato say to the baby tomato while they were out for a walk? Ketchup!

Why did the mushroom get invited to all the parties? Because he was such a fungi.

What's an astronaut's favourite hot drink? Gravi-tea.

French
Cheeses
by Cam M. Bert

Vegetables
by Arty Choke

Lunch
by Amelia Eatt

How to
Cook Steak
by
Carney Vore

Classic Pizza Toppings
by Anne Chovy

French Cookery
by Sue Flay

The Empty Biscuit Tin
by Arthur Anymore

Healthy Snacks
by Hazel Nutt

English Cheeses
by Wensley Dale

What's a skeleton's favourite barbecue?
Spare ribs.

Waiter, there's a button in my soup.
Thank you, sir. I've been looking for that everywhere.

Why are cooks cruel?
Because they beat eggs, whip cream and batter fish.

Why did the man throw his toast out of the window?
To watch his butterfly.

Mum: Why are you eating so fast?
Ali: I don't want to lose my appetite.

What do golfers eat for lunch?
Club sandwiches.

Waiter, bring me some lamb chops and make them lean.
To the left or right, sir?

Waiter, there's a spider drowning in my soup.
I don't think it's deep enough for him to drown, sir.

WRITE YOUR OWN TASTY JOKE...

How do you make
a lemon drop?
Let go of it.

Why was the
biscuit sad?
Because her mum
was a-wafer so long.

What did the grapes say when the
elephant stepped on them?
Nothing – they just let
out a little whine.

Why did the banana
go to the doctor?
Because it wasn't
peeling well.

Why was the onion stressed out?
Because it was in a pickle.

How do you make
a milkshake?
Show it a scary movie!

What do you
give a sick lemon?
Lemon-aid.

Why do French people
like to eat snails?
Because they don't
like fast food.

What's the hardest part about being an octopus?
Washing your hands before dinner.

How do you fix a broken pizza?
With tomato paste.

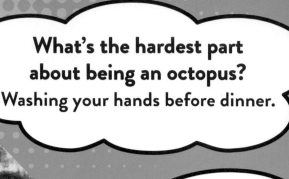

Why did the little girl put chocolate under her pillow?
She wanted sweet dreams.

What did the cake say to the fork?
You want a piece of me?

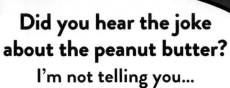

Did you hear the joke
about the peanut butter?
I'm not telling you...
you might spread it!

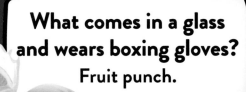

What comes in a glass
and wears boxing gloves?
Fruit punch.

What do you call a
bear with no teeth?
A gummy bear.

Where can you
learn how to
make ice cream?
Sundae School.

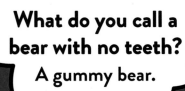

What's yellow and points north?
A magnetic banana.

What's black, white, green and bumpy?
A pickle in a tuxedo.

Knock, knock.
Who's there?
Broccoli.
Broccoli who?
Broccoli doesn't have a last name, silly!

What's a frog's favourite hot drink?
Croak-o.

How do you stop a rotten tomato from smelling? You pinch its nose.

Why did the can crusher quit his job? Because it was soda pressing.

What's a penguin's favourite salad? Iceberg lettuce.

Why did the T. rex only eat raw meat? Because it didn't know how to cook!

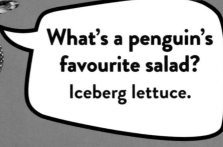

What do you call a crate of ducks? A box of quackers.

What's yellow, red and white and flies at 500 miles per hour?
A pilot's egg-and-tomato sandwich.

Why are eggs losers?
Because they're always beaten.

Waiter! This coffee tastes like mud!
I'm not surprised, miss, it was ground just a few minutes ago.

What did the bacon say to the egg?
I might be a ham, but your yolks are bad.

Have you heard the one about the giant fruit cake? It's very hard to swallow.

Knock, knock.
Who's there?
Bean.
Bean who?
Bean ages since I saw you!

Why can't you keep a secret on a farm?
Because the corn has ears and the potatoes have eyes.

Knock, knock.
Who's there?
Figs.
Figs who?
Figs your doorbell, it's broken!

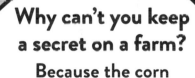

GROSS

Why did the girl take her nose apart?
She wanted to see what made it run.

What's brown on the outside, green on the inside, and hops?
A frog sandwich.

Knock, knock.
Who's there?
Earwig.
Earwig who?
Ear we go again!

What do you get if you cross a skunk with an owl?
A creature that smells, but doesn't give a hoot!

What do you call little white things in your head that bite?
Teeth.

What's green and hangs off trees?
Giraffe snot.

What do you call a worm in a fur coat?
A caterpillar.

Why did the bogey cross the road?
He was getting picked on.

55

Did you hear the story of the three eggs?
Two bad.

Knock, knock.
Who's there?
Ooze.
Ooze who?
Ooze eaten all the sweets?

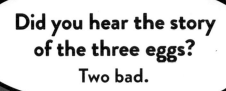

What's lumpy and smells like zebra?
Lion sick.

What did one maggot say to the other maggot?
Let's see you worm your way out of this one.

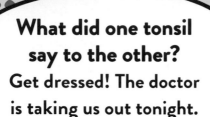

What did one tonsil
say to the other?
Get dressed! The doctor
is taking us out tonight.

What's the
difference between
roast chicken
and pea soup?
Anyone can
roast chicken.

Knock, knock.
Who's there?
A titch.
A titch who?
Bless you!

What do you get
if you cross a skunk
and a bear?
I don't know,
but it always gets
a seat on the bus!

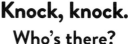

I have a green nose, three red mouths and four purple ears. What am I?
Ugly!

Why do golf players wear two pairs of underpants?
In case they get a hole in one.

What do you call someone who wipes their nose on their clothes?
Greensleeves.

Knock, knock.
Who's there?
Ken.
Ken who?
Ken you please open the door, I'm dying to go to the toilet!

Why did the man put an eye in the freezer?
He wanted to make an eye-cicle.

What bug can fly underwater?
A mosquito in a submarine.

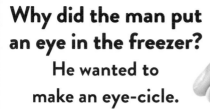

What can you keep even when you give it away?
A cold.

What's invisible and smells like carrots?
Rabbit farts.

What's a two-handed cheese?
One that you eat with one hand while you hold your nose with the other.

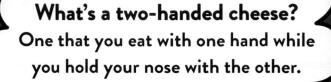

What did the slug say as he slipped down the wall?
How slime flies!

Waiter! This food's not fit for a pig!
I'll bring you some that is, sir.

What do you get if you're hit on the head with an axe?
A splitting headache.

What do sporty fleas watch at the weekend?
A football scratch.

Why was the sand wet?
Because the sea weed.

What do you get if you cross a birthday cake with a tin of baked beans?
A cake that blows out its own candles.

Knock, knock.
Who's there?
Butter.
Butter who?
Butter be quick, I need to go to the toilet.

Waiter! This egg is bad!
Don't blame me, sir, I only laid the table!

How do you know your kitchen floor is dirty?
The slugs leave a trail on the floor that reads, 'Clean me!'

What's yellow and gooey and smells like bananas?
Monkey snot.

Knock, knock.
Who's there?
Anita.
Anita who?
Anita tissue quick!

I do a really
good impression
of a bird...
I eat worms.

Help! A shark's just
bitten off my foot!
Which one?
How should I know?
All sharks look
the same to me.

What do you get if you cross
a seagull with a parrot?
A bird that poos on your
head and then says sorry.

Waiter! What
is that fly doing
on my ice cream?
Learning to ski, sir.

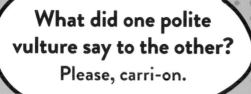

What did one polite vulture say to the other?
Please, carri-on.

What happens if you give your mouse some smelly cheese?
You make an awful mess of your computer.

Knock, knock.
Who's there?
Amos.
Amos who?
A mosquito just bit me!

Why was the nose so tired?
Because it had been running all day.

My brother must be built upside down. His nose runs and his feet smell.

I'm not sure what to give my sister for Christmas. Last year I gave her chicken pox.

Knock, knock.
Who's there?
Claire.
Claire who?
Claire out all this mess, I'm trying to get in!

What's brown and sticky?
A stick.

Knock, knock.
Who's there?
Weevil.
Weevil who?
Weevil have to go away if you don't open up!

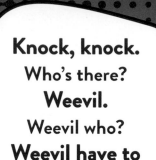

Is your bad tooth better now?
I don't know, I left it with the dentist.

What's the difference between Brussels sprouts and snot?
Children don't eat Brussels sprouts.

How can you stop your nose running?
Stick out your foot and trip it up.

Knock, knock.
Who's there?
Sonia.
Sonia who?
Sonia shoe, I can smell it from here!

Waiter! What's this fly doing in my soup?
Front crawl, I think.

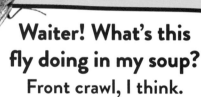

What's short, green and goes camping?
A boy sprout.

Why did the little girl bring her pet skunk to school?
For show-and-smell.

How do you start a bug race?
One, two, flea – go!

What's a mushroom?
A place where school
dinners are prepared.

Do you always wash in dirty water?
It wasn't dirty when I started.

Why are teenage
geese shy?
Because they get
goose pimples.

73

What do you call
a woman with two
toilets on her head?
Lulu.

How many farts
does it take to make
a stink bomb?
A phew!

How do fleas
get around?
They itch hike.

Where does
a burger bar
owner go
on holiday?
Greece.

74

What do you get if you cross a skunk with a boomerang?
A bad smell that keeps coming back.

How do you catch dandruff?
Shake your head over a paper bag!

What do you call a homeless snail?
A slug.

FOR SALE

Have you read that book about the skunk?
Don't bother – it stinks!

75

MONSTERS

What would you call a friendly monster?
A failure.

Why did the vampire become an artist?
Because he was so good at drawing blood.

What is Dracula's favourite fruit?
Neck-tarines.

How does a monster count to thirteen?
On her fingers.

What's a ghost's favourite ice cream flavour?
Shock-olate chip.

Why can you always tell a mummy your secret?
It'll keep it under wraps.

What does a witch ask for when she stays at a hotel?
Broom service.

Why didn't the skeleton go bungee jumping?
He didn't have the guts.

What do you call
a scared tree?
Petrified wood.

What do ghosts
do at Christmas?
They go to a
phantomime.

What did the ghost say
to the vampire?
Do you believe in people?

Why did the boy carry
a clock and a budgie
at Halloween?
So that he could go
tick or tweeting.

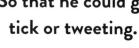

Why do witches use brooms to fly on?
Because vacuum cleaners are too heavy.

What's Dracula's favourite page in the newspaper?
The horror-scope.

What do vampires read their children at night?
Bite-time stories.

What kind of roads do ghosts haunt?
Dead ends.

WRITE YOUR OWN MONSTER JOKE...

Who sells cookies to monsters?
The Ghoul Scouts.

Who did Frankenstein take to the Halloween party?
His ghoul friend.

What do you call a fat jack-o-lantern?
A plumpkin.

Which room does a ghost like haunting the most?
The living room.

What do you get if you cross a cocker spaniel, a poodle and a ghost?
A cocker poodle boo.

What is Dracula's favourite ice cream?
Veinilla.

Which monster plays the most April Fool's jokes?
Prankenstein.

What do short-sighted ghosts wear?
Spook-tacles.

81

What happened when the witch met the wizard? It was love at first fright.

What has webbed feet and fangs? Count Quackula.

What do you get if you cross a plane with a wizard? A flying sorcerer.

What does Dracula do at eleven o'clock every morning? He takes a coffin break.

Do zombies eat popcorn with their fingers?
No, they eat the fingers separately.

Why couldn't Dracula's wife get to sleep?
Because of his coffin.

What's a vampire's favourite dance?
The fang-dango.

What do you call a vampire that lives in the kitchen?
Count Spatula.

What do you call a ghost who haunts the town hall?
A night mayor.

Where do monsters live?
In a monstro-city.

What kind of monster loves to dance?
A boogieman.

How do monsters like their eggs?
Terri-fried.

Where did the mum monster take her baby while she was at work? The day-scare centre.

What game do bats like to play at Halloween? Anything with a ball.

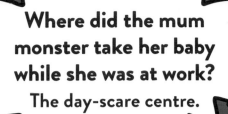

What did the alien say to the school librarian? Take me to your reader.

Why wouldn't the ghost cross the road? He had no guts.

Did you hear about the skeleton whose left arm and leg fell off?
He's all right now.

Where do skeletons like to swim?
In the Dead Sea.

Why did the monster knit herself three socks?
Because she grew another foot!

What is a vampire's favourite kind of coffee?
De-coffin-ated.

What did the thirsty skeleton
buy at the shop?
A drink and a mop.

First monster:
That girl just rolled
her eyes at me.
Second monster:
You'd better roll
them back, then.

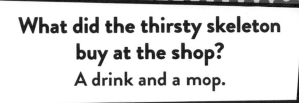

Why don't ghosts
go to discos?
They have no body
to dance with.

What does Dracula
say when he's
introduced to
someone new?
Pleased to eat you!

WRITE YOUR OWN GHOULISH JOKE...

What has a purple spotted body, ten hairy legs and big eyes on stalks?
I don't know either, but there's one crawling up your leg!

How can you tell when a vampire has been in a bakery?
All the jam has been sucked out of the jam doughnuts.

Why did the monster go into hospital?
To have his ghoul-stones removed.

What's a monster's favourite meal?
Ghoul-ash.

Why were the skeleton's teeth chattering?
She was chilled to the bone.

Why do ghosts always hang around in threes?
Because two's company, three's a shroud.

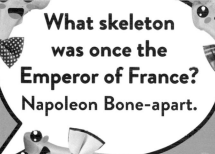

What skeleton was once the Emperor of France?
Napoleon Bone-apart.

What happened when the werewolf swallowed a clock?
He got ticks.

Why do you always find ghouls and demons together?
Because demons are a ghoul's best friend.

What are twin vampires called?
Blood brothers.

How do undertakers speak?
Gravely.

Why do monsters forget what you tell them?
Because it goes in one ear and out of all the others.

What do Italian ghosts like for dinner?
Spook-hetti.

How does an undertaker start a letter?
Tomb it may concern...

What did Frankenstein's monster say when he was struck by lightning?
I needed that.

What day of the week do monsters eat people?
Chewsday.

91

What do skeletons say before they eat?
Bone appetite!

What's Dracula's second favourite fruit?
Blood oranges.

Where are yetis found?
They're so big it's difficult to lose them.

Why did the skeleton feel the cold so badly?
The wind blew straight through him.

Why was the weather witch so unpopular? She was always forecasting sunny spells.

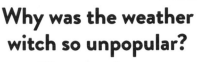

Doctor, I think I've been bitten by a vampire. Drink this glass of water. Will it make me better? No, but I'll be able to see if your neck leaks.

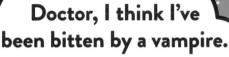

What do you get if you cross a snowman with a vampire? Frostbite.

What did the sea monster say when it saw a submarine? Ugh, I'm sick of tinned food!

Horror Stories
by R. U. Afraid

Ghostly Tales
by Ann Apparition

Vampire's Victim
by E. Drew Blood

Encyclopedia of Monsters by I. M. Scared

Werewolf Attack by Lucinda Woods

One Spooky Night by Hal O. Ween

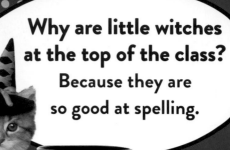

Why are little witches at the top of the class?
Because they are so good at spelling.

Why is the air so fresh and clean at Halloween?
Because of all the witches sweeping the sky.

How does a Martian keep his trousers up?
With an asteroid belt.

Why do witches have to stay calm when they're on a broomstick?
They don't want to fly off the handle.

Why did the witch give up fortune-telling? She couldn't see a future in it.

Why was the skeleton so mean? He didn't have a heart.

What goes around a haunted house and never stops? A fence.

What's a skeleton's favourite kind of art? Skull-pture.

Where do ghost trains stop?
At manifestations.

Where can you buy haunted food?
At the ghost-ery store.

What did the monster say to its victim?
Nice gnawing you!

Why don't vampires get fat?
They eat necks to nothing.

What shoes does a witch wear in the summer?
Open-toad sandals.

What has six legs and flies?
A witch and her cat on a broomstick.

What did the Martian chef find in his cupboard?
An unidentified frying object.

Who do ghosts invite to their parties?
Polter-guests.

WRITE YOUR OWN SPOOKY JOKE...

What did the ghost say after she had been out haunting all night?
I'm dead on my feet.

Why are Martians good at gardening?
Because they have green fingers.

How did the sick witch get to hospital?
She flu.

Why are skeletons so calm?
Because nothing gets under their skin.

Why did the woman
spend day and night
learning how to cast spells?
She wanted to
get witch quick.

What happens in
a haunted theatre?
The actors get stage fright.

What do giants do for fun?
Tell each other tall stories.

What do owls do
at Halloween?
They have a hoot.

Josh: How old is Mr Pratt?
Sam: Really old.
He told me he used to teach Shakespeare!

Teacher: Name five fruits.
Toby: One apple and four oranges!

Why is six afraid of seven?
Because seven ate nine.

Why shouldn't you write with a blunt pencil?
There's no point.

Knock, knock.
Who's there?
Ivana.
Ivana who?
Ivana come in, open the door!

How does a broom act? With sweeping gestures.

Where do polar bears come from? Chilly.

What has two hands but no arms? A clock.

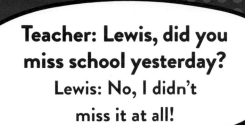

Teacher: Lewis, did you
miss school yesterday?
Lewis: No, I didn't
miss it at all!

What did one candle
say to the other?
Shall we go out tonight?

What is a sleeping bag?
A nap-sack.

What's black
and white and
red all over?
A newspaper.

What is a maths teacher's favourite dessert? Pi.

What do you call a Victorian bug? An ant-ique.

What lies at the bottom of the sea and trembles? A nervous wreck.

Teacher: Is eating chicken good for your health? Dan: Not if you're a chicken!

How do mountains hear? With their mountaineers.

Alex: Dad, can you help me find the answer for my maths homework?
Dad: Is it still missing? I remember looking for it when I was at school!

What do you call a pen with no hair?
A bald point.

What's a bird's favourite subject?
Owl-gebra.

What's the difference between a train and a tree?
One leaves its shed and the other sheds its leaves.

Teachers are always telling pupils to follow their dreams.
Yet they complain if they sleep in class!

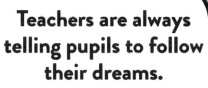

What kind of nut do you hang pictures on?
A walnut.

What did the snowball do when it stopped rolling?
Looked round.

Dad: Why aren't you doing very well in history?
George: Because the teacher keeps asking me about things that happened before I was born!

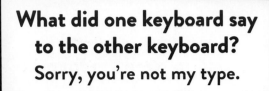

What did one keyboard say to the other keyboard?
Sorry, you're not my type.

What did the dinosaur have for lunch at school?
The head teacher.

Knock, knock.
Who's there?
A little old lady.
A little old lady who?
I didn't know you could yodel.

What is small, white and goes up?
A confused snowflake.

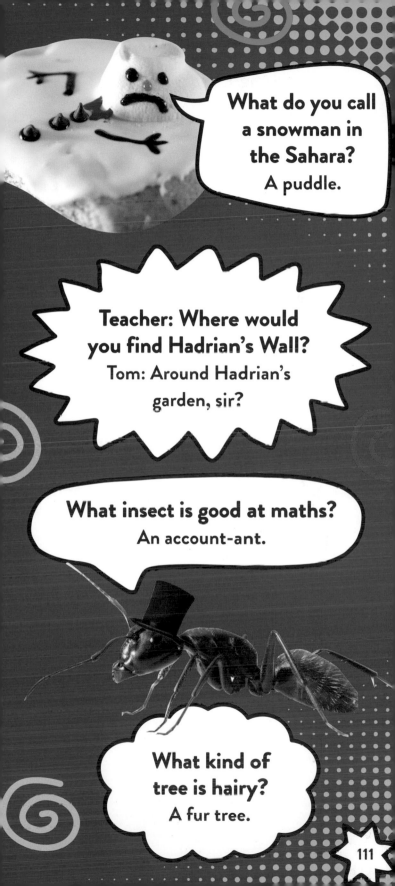

What do you call a snowman in the Sahara?
A puddle.

Teacher: Where would you find Hadrian's Wall?
Tom: Around Hadrian's garden, sir?

What insect is good at maths?
An account-ant.

What kind of tree is hairy?
A fur tree.

111

When does money
fall out of the sky?
Whenever there's change
in the weather.

Charlie: I've been banned
from cookery lessons because
I burned something.
Mum: What did you burn?
Charlie: I burned the school down.

Teacher: Did the
ancient Romans
hunt bear?
Edward: Not in
the winter, if they
had any sense!

Harvey: How many
teachers work
at this school?
Henry: About
half of them!

What is everyone's favourite tree?
A poplar.

Dad: What did you learn in school today?
Daniel: I learned that those sums you did for me were wrong.

What's the fastest country in the world?
Rush-a.

Teacher: What happened at the Boston Tea Party?
Grace: I don't know, I wasn't invited.

113

Teacher: Why don't you write more neatly?

James: Because then you'll be able to see that I can't spell!

Alfred: Mum, please don't make me go to school today. I hate it!

Mum: You have to go – you're the headmaster!

Why was the teacher cross-eyed? She couldn't control her pupils.

Music teacher: What would you like to play?

Joe: Truant!

What country do ponies come from? Horse-tralia.

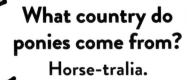

Dad: How were the exam questions?
Molly: Fine.
Dad: Why are you crying, then?
Molly: The questions were fine. The answers were the problem.

How did the Vikings send secret messages?
By Norse code.

What has five eyes and runs for over two thousand miles?
The Mississippi River.

Teacher: That story's excellently written for someone your age!
Ella: How about for someone my mum's age?

Teacher: I hear you've been telling everyone I'm boring.
Harry: Sorry, I didn't know it was meant to be a secret.

Why did the chicken cross the playground? To get to the other slide.

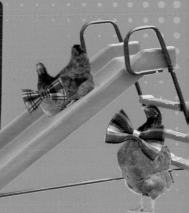

Who would you find on a beach at Halloween? Sand-witches.

Teacher: Why are a lot of famous artists Dutch?
Tom: Because they were born in Holland!

Arctic Ocean
by Isa Berg

**Snakes
of the World**
by Anna Conda

**Learn to
Speed Read**
by Paige Turner

Building Robots
by Anne Droid

Sports Day
by Arthur Letics

Almost Missed
the Bus
by Justin Time

End of the Week
by Gladys Friday

Teacher: Why can't you answer any of my questions?
Emily: Well, if I could there wouldn't be much point in me being here!

Why do windows squeak when you open them? Because they have panes.

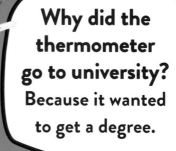

Why did the thermometer go to university? Because it wanted to get a degree.

Teacher: If you put your hand in your left pocket and found £1.75, then put your hand in your right pocket and found £2.50, what would you have?
Harry: Somebody else's trousers on!

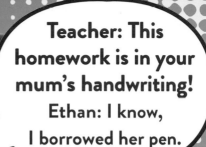

Teacher: This homework is in your mum's handwriting!
Ethan: I know, I borrowed her pen.

Why did the man run around his bed? He was trying to catch up on his sleep.

Why is Ireland so rich? Because its capital is always Dublin.

Jack: My teacher's an angel.
Alfie: You're lucky. Mine's still alive!

Teacher: What is a duchess?
Joe: I dunno. Is it different from an English 's'?

121

Teacher: If I gave you three hamsters, and the next day gave you three more, how many would you have?
Ruby: Seven.
Teacher: Seven?
Ruby: Yes, I've got one already.

What's a snake's best subject?
Hiss-tory.

What's a bug's favourite subject?
Mothematics.

What do elves learn in school?
The elf-abet.

Teacher: Tell me an animal that lives in Lapland.
Charlie: A reindeer.
Teacher: Good, now tell me another one.
Charlie: Another reindeer!

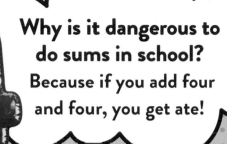

Why is it dangerous to do sums in school? Because if you add four and four, you get ate!

Teacher: If you had five pounds and you asked your dad for another five pounds, how much would you have? Jack: Five pounds. **Teacher: You don't know how to add up!** Jack: You don't know my dad.

How do dinosaurs pass exams? With extinction.

WRITE YOUR OWN LAUGH-OUT-LOUD JOKE...

Why isn't your nose 12 inches long? Because then it would be a foot.

Teacher: You've got your shoes on the wrong feet.
Adam: These are the only feet I've got, sir.

What do goblins drink with their school lunch?
Lemon 'n' slime.

Teacher: You're not paying attention – are you having trouble hearing?
Sophie: No, miss. I'm having trouble listening!

Why did the clock get angry?
It was wound up.

Where do wasps come from?
Sting-apore.

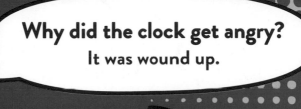

Why was the chimney ill?
It had the flue.

Teacher: I hope
I didn't see you looking
at Jack's answers!
Harry: I hope
you didn't, too.

Where do pigs come from?
Ham-erica.

Teacher: Dylan, stop humming while you're working!
Dylan: I'm not working, miss, just humming!

Teacher: What do you call a tree that loses its leaves?
Hannah: Careless?

What do you call the biggest bully in the playground?
Lord of the Swings.

Teacher: Name a liquid that will never freeze.
Samuel: Hot water.

How can you make seven even?
Take away the 's'.

Why was Cinderella dropped from the school football team?
Because she ran away from the ball.

Teacher: What time did you wake up this morning, Joe?
Joe: About 10 minutes after I got to school, sir!

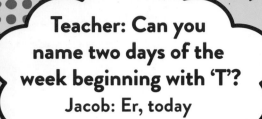

Teacher: Can you name two days of the week beginning with 'T'?
Jacob: Er, today and tomorrow?

What is the healthiest lesson? History, because it's full of dates.

What did the zero say to the eight? Nice belt.

Teacher: Which word is always spelled wrong?
Lily: Wrong?